LUDWIG VAN
BEETHOVEN

Richard Tames

Franklin Watts

London • New York • Sydney • Toronto

Contents

The Apprentice   **4**

Teachers of Genius   **9**

The Virtuoso   **10**

Eroica   **16**

The Master   **17**

"Wellington's Victory"   **22**

The Final Struggle   **24**

Beethoven and Britain   **29**

Find Out More ...   **30**

Glossary   **31**

Index   **32**

© Franklin Watts 1991

First published in Great Britain
in 1991 by
Franklin Watts
96 Leonard Street
London EC2A 4RH

First published in the USA by
Franklin Watts Inc.
387 Park Avenue South
New York, N.Y. 10016

First published in Australia by
Franklin Watts
14 Mars Road
Lane Cove
NSW 2066

UK ISBN: 0 7496 0265 1

Phototypeset by: JB Type, Hove, East Sussex
Printed in: Belgium
Series Editor: Hazel Poole
Designed by: Nick Cannan

A CIP catalogue record for this book is available from
the British Library.

The Apprentice

Many people think of Beethoven as the greatest composer who ever lived. His works include nine **symphonies**, an opera, two choral masses, 48 **sonatas**, 10 overtures and dozens of trios, quartets and songs. He was both a complete master of musical technique and an artist of great passion and striking originality. His example inspired other leading composers, who were proud to acknowledge their debt to him.

Beethoven's importance lies not only in his work but in his life. Before Beethoven, a composer worked to please a **patron**, amuse an audience or to serve the needs of religious worship. Beethoven wrote music simply for its own sake, and from that time on, the composer was recognized not as a servant or a craftsman, but as an artist in his own right.

Beethoven was called Ludwig after his grandfather (1712-73), who had left both the family bakery business and his native country of Flanders to become a professional musician in Germany. At that time, Germany was not one country but split into scores of small states ruled by kings, princes or bishops. Some of these states were no larger than a single city. The rulers of the

more important ones were entitled to help choose the Holy Roman Emperor who ruled in Vienna and was their superior ruler. Many of them also tried to imitate his grand court.

By the time he was 20, grandfather Ludwig, a fine bass singer, had been hired as a court musician by the Elector Clemens August, Archbishop of Cologne who governed from the small city of Bonn, a quiet and pleasant place which is now the capital of the Federal Republic of Germany (West Germany). In those days it had approximately 10,000 inhabitants, most of whom depended on the court in one way or another for

"My worthy grandfather" as Beethoven called him — a serious-minded and respected musician — unlike his son, Johann.

their living. Grandfather Ludwig was to spend the rest of his life in Bonn, working as a musician and selling wine as a side-line. Wine proved to be the downfall of his wife, Maria Josepha, who drank so much that she was placed in a convent. The gifted musician was left on his own to pursue his career at court, run his business and bring up his only son, Johann (1739-92).

Johann van Beethoven followed his father into the service of the Elector as a musician, first as a boy soprano, then as a tenor. His career seemed assured when in 1761 his father was appointed Kapellmeister (Master of the Chapel) — the chief musician at court. But in 1767 Johann, very much against his

The composer's birthplace (left), **an upper floor at Bonngasse 515. Beethoven's mother** (above), **stable, gentle and affectionate — a complete contrast to his father.**

father's wishes, chose to marry the young widowed daughter of the senior cook at the palace. Perhaps they hoped it would reconcile the old man to their marriage when they chose the name Ludwig for their son born on December 16, 1770. Johann proved to be neither as good a husband nor as talented a musician as his father. When the Kapellmeister died in 1773, Johann and his young family lost a powerful, if grumpy, friend and protector.

The old organ in Beethoven's house. He was appointed assistant court organist at the age of 11.

As a growing boy in a small city, Ludwig van Beethoven could scarcely fail to hear how highly respected his grandfather had been. Throughout his life he treasured the memory of "my worthy grandfather" and kept his portrait hanging on the wall as an inspiration. The contrast with his unsuccessful father could scarcely have been more striking. Once his father had died, Johann failed to progress at court, mismanaged the family finances and seemed quite unable to settle down in one home for any length of time. He also seemed to have inherited his mother's taste for drink.

As young Ludwig grew up, even his father could see that he had exceptional musical talent. Johann knew that Leopold Mozart was making a small fortune out of his remarkable son, Wolfgang, by getting him to perform at courts throughout Germany. Why not use his own gifted offspring in the same way? In 1778, Johann organized a concert for young Ludwig. To make his talent seem all the more brilliant Johann proclaimed that Ludwig was only six; in fact he was eight. But the concert failed to launch a glittering new career.

Little Ludwig was not a natural show-off like the young Mozart, and Johann certainly had none of Leopold Mozart's shrewdness as a businessman.

Ludwig's schooling stopped when it meant paying for lessons. Bonn had a free school, but Ludwig had to leave in 1781 when he passed the age limit. He never did learn to spell correctly, write neatly or calculate accurately. All his efforts went into music.

Fortunately for the young Beethoven, a new court organist, Christian Gottlob Neefe (1748-98), was appointed in 1782. Within a year, Neefe declared that "This youthful genius is deserving of help to enable him to travel. He would surely become a second Wolfgang Amadeus Mozart were he to continue as he has begun."

Beethoven benefited from Neefe's training but received no salary until April 1784, when he was appointed second organist. He did, however, begin to earn money by teaching music to the children of Frau von Breuning, the widow of a court official. The von Breuning family were both kindly and cultured. They welcomed the rather clumsy and scruffy teenager, introduced him to polite society, lent him books and in many other ways helped to make up for the education he had missed.

In 1787, thanks to Neefe's help, Beethoven was given money to take him 500 miles away to the great city of Vienna, where he could learn

Beethoven's first teacher, Neefe, himself began composing at the age of 12.

much from the most outstanding musicians of his day. Almost as soon as he arrived, Beethoven had the chance to play for Mozart. The great **virtuoso** was far less impressed by Beethoven's playing than by his ability to improvise. Mozart was not so obsessed by his own extraordinary powers that he could not recognize genius in others. "Keep your eye on him," he told his friends, "some day he will give the world something to talk about." Mozart, however, died shortly afterwards and never took Beethoven on as his pupil as had seemed possible after their meeting.

Less than two weeks after arriving in Vienna, Beethoven heard that his mother was seriously ill. He hurried back to nurse her but, despite every effort, she died in July at the age of 40. Before the end of the same year, Beethoven's baby sister had also died. His father went downhill even faster than before, neglecting his work and drinking heavily. Beethoven gave up all hope of returning to Vienna and took over the responsibility for his younger brothers, Carl Caspar and Nikolaus Johann. When his father's drunkenness got him into trouble with the police, Beethoven persuaded the court to let him take control of the family finances.

Beethoven now became the family's main source of income, playing the organ at the Elector's court and playing the viola in his new theatre. The von Breunings were still glad to see him and encouraged him to take courses at the new local university. They were also happy to observe that he was busy with composing, even though he had still not had anything published.

In 1790, the Emperor, Joseph II, died and when a local poet wrote an ode in his memory, Beethoven set it to music as a **cantata**. The work was never actually performed in Beethoven's lifetime but he did show it to Joseph Haydn (1732-1809) when the great man passed through Bonn on his way back from England. Haydn was evidently impressed and agreed to accept Beethoven as a pupil. Once again money was found to send him off to Vienna, and one of his friends, Count Ferdinand Waldstein, assured Beethoven that if he worked hard he would surely "receive Mozart's spirit from Haydn's hands."

Bonn — the three-language hotel sign suggests an international atmosphere for a relatively small city.

Teachers of Genius

Beethoven's first teacher was his father, Johann. His methods were harsh and extreme. Sometimes, coming home drunk at night, he would haul the little boy out of bed to play for his friends.

Beethoven's real musical education began when the court organist, Neefe, took charge of him. Neefe taught him systematically, encouraged him to start composing, gave him responsibility and pushed hard to get him into the wider world of music outside of Bonn. Beethoven always acknowledged this debt and when he had become famous in Vienna, he wrote — "I thank you for the counsel which you gave me so often in my progress in my divine art. If ever I become a great man yours shall be a share of the credit."

In Vienna, Beethoven was grateful to take lessons from Haydn, who reported warmly on his progress to his patron, the Elector of Cologne — "... expert and amateur alike cannot but admit that Beethoven will in time become one of the greatest musical artists in Europe, and I shall be proud to call myself his teacher." But Beethoven began to find Haydn too easy-going and, although the two remained on good terms, he looked around for other instructors — and never referred to Haydn afterwards as one of his teachers. Antonio Salieri, Mozart's old enemy, taught Beethoven how to set vocal pieces, Johann Schenk gave him an insight into dramatic composition and Emanuel Aloys Förster showed him how to write for the string quartet.

It was Johann Georg Albrechtsberger who taught Beethoven the complex art of **counterpoint.** He was a tough disciplinarian and one might have expected the proud Beethoven to rebel against him, but Beethoven knew that he needed a strict instructor if he was to acquire a thorough understanding of the technical aspects of his art.

Joseph Haydn (1732-1809) — Mozart acknowledged him as a complete master of music.

The Virtuoso

Vienna had twenty times the population of Bonn and from the Emperor downwards, the Viennese were lovers of music. They not only hired musicians to perform for them but also commissioned composers to write new music, either for a special occasion like a wedding, or simply for their own amusement.

Beethoven arrived in Vienna with recommendations from influential people — his employer, the Elector, his friend Count Waldstein, and the great Haydn himself. But as yet no-one valued him as a composer. He made his mark as a piano virtuoso, capable of sight-reading the most difficult music instantly or of improvising for an hour on a theme suggested by a member of an audience. Mozart, the city's hero, had just died and Beethoven soon came to take the place he had vacated.

Beethoven's father died in 1792. In 1794, the armies of the revolutionary French republic invaded Bonn and the Elector of Cologne fled from the city, never to hold power there again. Carl Caspar Beethoven fled also and found his elder brother in Vienna, where the young maestro found him work as a music teacher. Nikolaus Johann joined them in 1795. He

Vienna c. 1790 — a great city but still only a few steps from the countryside.

Prince Karl Lichnowsky (1758-1814) was, like his brother and son, a generous and patient patron.

was a trained apothecary and, in later years, Ludwig was able to set him up in his own business in the town of Linz. Even if Beethoven had wanted to go back to Bonn, there was now neither court nor family for him to return to.

By 1795, Beethoven's reputation made him the star performer at great public concerts given to raise money for Mozart's widow and to honour the aged Haydn. In 1796, Beethoven went on tour, giving concerts in Prague, Dresden, Leipzig and Berlin, where the King of Prussia showed his appreciation by giving him a gold **snuff**-box filled with gold coins. Beethoven

had known enough of poverty to value the wealth he could earn from his skill at the piano. But he was not content to be a mere entertainer of the rich. Unlike most musicians before his time, he was not prepared to abase himself before patrons in the hope of gifts or a permanent court appointment. He was thoroughly convinced by the revolutionary ideas then sweeping through France that men and women should be valued for their talents, not their birth. He believed this to be particularly true of artists, for their gifts enriched not merely themselves but others as well.

Beethoven, therefore, expected his patrons to treat him as an equal and not as a servant, much less as a performing toy. He was fortunate that his first great patron, Prince Karl Lichnowsky (1756-1814), was a gracious and sensitive man, who fully appreciated the depth of Beethoven's emerging genius. Lichnowsky gave Beethoven an apartment in his palace and a quartet of fine string instruments. Beethoven himself declared that the Prince treated him like "a friend and a brother". But Beethoven could still be very difficult. When he heard that Lichnowsky had told his personal servant to take care of Beethoven even if it meant putting the Prince second, Beethoven went straight out and hired his own servant. The Prince did manage to deceive Beethoven — in the nicest possible

way — for it was Lichnowsky who paid for the costs of Beethoven's first published work, a set of three trios in 1795, although Beethoven believed that his income came from the successful sale of these works.

Beethoven's daily routine began with an early breakfast and then he spent the morning in either composition or teaching. He was too impatient and moody to be a good teacher. After lunch at noon he would go for a long walk, composing in his head and occasionally pausing to scribble down an idea.

Unlike Mozart, who seemed to have an extraordinary talent for getting things just right the first time, Beethoven often worked and re-worked his compositions again and again over a long period of time. His notebooks show clearly how he battled, sometimes for years, to bring a particular project to perfection. He did not publish his first symphony until he was 31 years old. By that age, Mozart had published over 40.

At the end of his walk, Beethoven would often stop at an inn to read a newspaper or have a drink with friends. Although he was often preoccupied with his music he was not an unsociable man. He enjoyed good company and the theatre. But if he wasn't performing in the evening he would often go to bed early, ready to start afresh the following dawn. Beethoven, again unlike Mozart, did not shine in society, and he knew it. When he first moved to Vienna he took dancing lessons, but made little progress. His appearance was also rather forbidding. Short, but powerfully built, he had a shock of wild hair and a **pockmarked** complexion. He dressed untidily and often went unshaven for days on end. In his manner he was often awkward, knocking things over and finding that even simple tasks, like making coffee or sharpening a quill pen, often proved a trial and were best left to servants or friends. As for his rooms, they were legendary for their chaos. Yet Beethoven did not lack friends, and many women found him strangely attractive. Six years in Vienna had made him famous, well-off and successful. Then he began to experience a strange buzzing sensation in his left ear.

Beethoven gave his first public concert in April 1800, selling the tickets himself from his own lodgings. The programme included items by the two great composers of the day, Mozart and Haydn. But mostly it was Beethoven — as composer of all the remaining

Increasing deafness made the composer unaware of other people around him.

items, as piano soloist and as conductor of his own First Symphony. The concert was a success but not an outstanding one. However, Beethoven's hearing difficulties had made him so worried that he began to consult a number of doctors.

In 1801, Beethoven took on Carl Czerny (1791-1857), who was to become his best-known pupil and who later became the teacher of the piano virtuoso and composer, Franz Liszt. Czerny, although only a boy of 10, vividly recalled his first meeting with his new master:

"a rather untidy looking servant announced us ... The room presented a most disorderly appearance — papers and articles of clothing were scattered about everywhere, some trunks, bare walls, hardly a chair ..."

The mess was not surprising. Beethoven lived in Vienna for 35 years — at 33 different addresses, not including his summer breaks in the surrounding countryside, which would add another 38 places. So he rarely bothered to unpack properly. Another of Beethoven's pupils was Ferdinand Ries (1784-1838) who turned up that same year almost penniless. The Ries family had helped Beethoven during his mother's last illness and in gratitude he took the son as a pupil and helped him out with money.

Czerny distinctly remembered that when he first met Beethoven "he did not give the least evidence of deafness" but he did notice "that he had cotton, which seemed to have been steeped in a yellowish liquid, in his ears." Beethoven had, at first, tried to ignore his growing deafness, appalled to think of what it would mean for him as a professional musician. But by July 1801, he was confessing in a letter to a friend that: "my noblest faculty, my hearing, has greatly deteriorated ... it is continually growing worse." He voiced his innermost fear, that the condition would be incurable and prevent him from "accomplishing all that my talent and powers bid me do", and concluded in desperation "I beg of you to keep the matter of my deafness a profound secret to be confided to nobody, no matter whom". In another letter, written to Franz Wegeler, a friend who was also a doctor, Beethoven described the effects of his illness on his life:

"My ears sing and buzz continually, day and night. I can truly say that I am leading a wretched life. For two years I have avoided almost all social gatherings because it is impossible for me to say to people "I am deaf." If I belonged to any other profession it would be easier, but in my profession it is a frightful state."

Beethoven explained that his deafness was by no means total, but that he had difficulty hearing high notes and softly-spoken voices. Uncertain whether the condition could even be arrested, let alone cured, Beethoven wavered between moods of defiance and despair. In April 1802, following medical advice to live in a quiet place, Beethoven moved to the village of Heiligenstadt, where he stayed until the autumn. On the eve of his return to Vienna for the winter he wrote a long document which has become known as the "Heiligenstadt Testament". Although composed in the form of a letter to his brothers it was never actually sent, but a copy was found among his papers after his death. Perhaps by writing down all his worst fears, Beethoven hoped to get control of them. The rambling "Testament" certainly presents a picture of a man frustrated and tormented by cruel fortune:

"Oh you men who think or say that I am malevolent, stubborn or **misanthropic**, how greatly do you wrong me. You do not know the

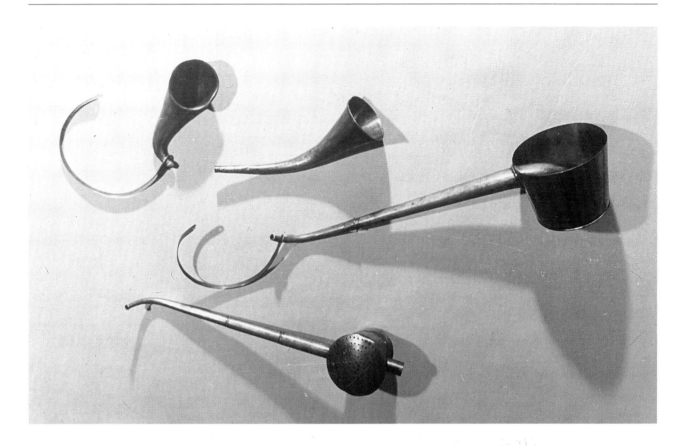

Hearing aids designed to help the composer overcome his deafness.

secret which makes me seem that way to you. From childhood on my heart and soul have been full of the tender feelings of goodwill and I was ever inclined to accomplish great things. But ... I have been hopelessly afflicted, made worse by senseless physicians, from year to year deceived with hopes of improvement."

Beethoven wrote many pages about his loneliness, his pain at being shunned and misunderstood by friends whose company he longed for, and his grief at the loss of a sense of hearing "which I once possessed in the highest perfection, a perfection such as few in my profession enjoy ..."

He addressed his brothers, forgiving past wrongs, advising them how to bring up their children, leaving them his "small fortune" to share between them and asking them to let people know about his affliction so that they would at last understand and forgive his strange behaviour. He even remembered to thank Prince Lichnowsky for his generosity.

Despite the mental turmoil revealed in this sad composition, Beethoven managed during the summer of 1802 to complete his Second symphony, a work noted for its sunny and optimistic tone. His determination had conquered his desperation and he entered a period of intense musical activity.

Eroica

Beethoven's Third symphony (1803) is sometimes thought to be the one in which he first wrote in a style quite recognizably his own, rather than based on that of a previous composer. It was twice as long as any symphony written by Mozart or Haydn and thus challenged the basic idea of what a symphony should or could be.

As a believer in talent, effort and courage, Beethoven had come to admire the brilliant young general who had repeatedly led the armies of revolutionary France to victory — Napoleon Bonaparte. By 1802, Napoleon had defeated every major power in Europe and even the French republic's implacable enemy, Britain, had signed an **armistice**. By early 1804, the new composition was finished and Beethoven announced his intention to dedicate it to Bonaparte. But Bonaparte himself had an announcement to make just then — that the French republic was over and that he would make himself Emperor of the French. Beethoven at once saw him in a new and unflattering light — as a man of naked personal ambition, not a selfless reformer, fighting for the liberation of oppressed peoples.

The surviving manuscript of what Beethoven had called the *Sinfonia Grande Intitulata Bonaparte* has a hole in the paper where the composer violently rubbed out the last two words. Instead it was re-dedicated to a patron, Prince Lobkowitz, and published with the haughty inscription "to celebrate the memory of a great man". Beethoven's Third symphony is now know as *Eroica* — heroic — and the name is well-chosen, for it evokes power and restless energy, well-fitted to the character of a hero.

Napoleon — the hero who became a villain to Beethoven, an ardent lover of liberty.

The Master

In 1803, the owner of the new Theater-an-der-Wien, the largest in all Vienna, offered Beethoven the position of composer in residence, with the right to conduct a concert in the theatre whenever he chose and the obligation to write a new opera to be performed there.

Beethoven's concert, performed in April 1803, included both his First and Second symphonies, his Third piano concerto, and a new oratorio, *Christ on the Mount of Olives*, written especially for the occasion. As was usual with Beethoven, everything was something of a muddle. At five o'clock on the morning of the concert, Beethoven was found sitting up in bed, still writing out trombone parts for the orchestra. Rehearsals began at eight and soon dissolved into chaos. Fortunately, the ever-indulgent Prince Lichnowsky, who sat right through the rehearsals, paid for food and wine to be brought in for everyone in an effort to calm things down. When it came to the concert itself, Beethoven played most of the piano part of the oratorio entirely from memory, having had no time to write out his own part.

After the concert came his only opera. Beethoven decided to base it on a French play, *Leonore, or Conjugal Love*, by J. N. Bouilly, which was translated into German for him. Today Beethoven's opera is known as *Fidelio*. The story tells of a woman, Leonore, who determines to rescue her innocent husband, Florestan, from prison, before the prison governor, Pizarro, can have him killed to settle an old grudge. Disguised as a young man, Fidelio, Leonore goes to work in the prison and finds herself having to dig a grave for her husband, who is about

The imposing facade of the large and elegant Theater-an-der-Wien, the grandest in Vienna.

A dramatic moment during the third act of *Fidelio*

to be murdered. Pulling out a pistol to fend off the evil Pizarro, she and her husband are rescued at the crucial moment by the sudden arrival of the Prime Minister, Don Fernando, who then ensures that Florestan is released and Pizarro arrested.

Beethoven was attracted by the powerful themes of the story, those of injustice defeated, courage vindicated and the power of love to overcome even the most forbidding perils. He set out to finish the work in six months — it took him two years.

At the time that *Leonore* (as it was first known) was being rehearsed, the French army, having defeated the Austrians at the battle of Ulm, was occupying Vienna. Beethoven was still not satisfied with his opera, substituting an entirely new overture for the one he had originally written. At the very last moment, the theatre manager decided to change the title as well, substituting *Fidelio* for *Leonore*. The premiere attracted only a small audience, which consisted mainly of French soldiers, who were unable to understand any German. There were only three performances before the opera was taken off.

In December 1805, Prince

Lichnowsky and his friends got together and went through *Fidelio* in detail, persuading the composer that it was far too long and needed drastic cuts. Beethoven relented and made them. Then he restored them and made others. Then he re-wrote the opening overture entirely. Cut from three acts to two, it was performed again in 1806 but only twice. The critics preferred it, but Beethoven was furious because he thought that the orchestra played badly, and that the theatre was cheating him of his share of the takings.

The failure of *Fidelio* turned Beethoven away from the profitable path of opera. His worsening deafness would deny him an income from performing, conducting or teaching. How would he earn his living? Many musicians competed for the favour of a patron, but Beethoven was seldom prepared to put himself out. In 1806, he quarrelled with Prince Lichnowsky when he was asked to improvise for some French officers who were his guests. Beethoven did not feel like performing to order and stormed out of the house. In 1807, Prince Nikolaus Esterhazy, Haydn's former patron, asked Beethoven to compose a special Mass. Beethoven, unusually, managed to finish the commission on time. But when he went to the Prince's palace to conduct the new work he was treated in an off-hand way and his music failed to please. Embittered, Beethoven refused to hand over the score — and lost another possible patron.

In 1808, Beethoven turned down an offer to become Kapellmeister to Jerôme Bonaparte, King of the newly-established state called Westphalia. But the very thought that Beethoven might abandon Vienna was enough to prompt three patrons "to place Herr Ludwig van Beethoven in a position where the necessaries of life shall not cause him embarrassment," by providing him with an annual pension of 4,000 **florins** a year for life. The three patrons were the Archduke Rudolph (1788-1832), brother to the Emperor himself and a pupil of Beethoven's since 1803, another

Prince Nikolaus Esterhazy (1765-1833), proud and wealthy patron of Haydn.

young nobleman, Prince Kinsky (1781-1812) and an old friend, Prince Lobkowitz (1772-1816). It was an even more generous arrangement than Jerôme had offered — a higher income and no tiresome duties running an orchestra.

Beethoven had little time, however, to enjoy his new security. The first payment of his pension came in February 1809. By May, the Emperor and his family had fled the city and the French army was besieging it. Beethoven took refuge in the cellar of the house of his brother, Carl Caspar, where he lay miserably, with cushions over his head, trying to protect his ears from the thud and screaming of artillery shells. He wrote wretchedly that life seemed to consist of "nothing but drums, cannons and human misery in every form."

Austria's humiliation at the hands of France plunged Beethoven into further money worries. Defeat led to a collapse in the value of Austrian currency, which reduced Beethoven's handsome pension to a fraction of its former worth. Archduke Rudolph did increase his share to a decent sum, but Kinsky was killed in a riding accident in 1812 and Lobkowitz was so nearly bankrupt that he couldn't pay anything for four years. Money was to remain a problem for Beethoven for the rest of his life. Arithmetic had never been his strongest subject and as he grew more deaf he grew more distrustful, always thinking that people were out to cheat him.

Beethoven's personal circumstances also remained uncomfortable. A French visitor who called on him in 1809 described his living room:

"Picture to yourself the dirtiest, most disorderly place imaginable — blotches of damp covered the ceiling ... under the piano ... an unemptied chamber pot; beside it, a small walnut table accustomed to the frequent overturning of materials placed upon it; a quantity of pens encrusted with ink ... chairs ... covered with plates bearing the remains of last night's supper ..."

Family ties offered some

Carl Czerny (1791-1857) a devoted pupil and composer of 1,000 works.

compensation to Beethoven for his isolation and discomfort, but they were far from stable and secure. Beethoven's brother, Carl Caspar, had married Johanna Reiss, the daughter of a well-off craftsman, in 1806. Beethoven did not approve and quarrelled with his brother but they soon became reconciled after the birth of his nephew, Karl. Beethoven himself would dearly have liked to marry but, although he was often in love, never found the right woman. In 1810, he proposed to Therese Malfatti, the teenage daughter of his doctor. She admired his music but had no wish to become his wife. In 1812, Beethoven fell in love with an unnamed lady, perhaps the wife of a friend, known only as the "Eternally Beloved", whose identity is still not clear and probably never will be. In any case, Beethoven's passion was confined to long love letters. In 1812, Beethoven's other brother, Nikolaus Johann, married his housekeeper. Beethoven didn't consider her a suitable wife either and another quarrel resulted.

"Wellington's Victory"

Napoleon's amazing luck began to run out with his disastrous attack on Russia in 1812. The following year a British army under the Duke of Wellington defeated the French occupation forces in Spain at the battle of Vittoria. In October of the same year, Russia, Prussia, Austria and Sweden joined together to defeat Napoleon himself at Leipzig. Austrians now had something to cheer about and one of Beethoven's fellow-Viennese saw a way to cash in on their patriotic pride. Johann Mälzel (1772-1838) was the ingenious inventor of the "Mechanical Panharmonicon", a sort of cross between a fairground organ and a primitive juke-box, which could imitate a military band. Mälzel had come to know Beethoven from making ear-trumpets for him and suggested that he should write something lively and topical for his magic machine.

Beethoven obliged with a piece celebrating Wellington's victory at Vittoria and bringing snatches of well-known tunes associated with Britain and France. Mälzel then suggested re-writing the piece so that it could be played by a

Wellington (top left, fourth from left) **supervises his major victory.**

proper orchestra at a public concert to raise money for the widows and orphans of Austrian soldiers. As it was for charity, Beethoven agreed and many of Vienna's leading musicians offered their services as well. Although Beethoven's composition was, by his own high standards, pretty dismal, it seemed to be popular with the public. Beethoven grew so enthusiastic at this unexpected triumph that he dismissed Mälzel and held a second successful concert. Mälzel, not surprisingly, got himself a lawyer and tried to get a share of the profits of an idea which had been his in the first place. Beethoven refused to compromise and when Mälzel produced two performances of it for his own benefit Beethoven sued him — also without result.

As usual with Beethoven's quarrels, it all ended happily enough when tempers had cooled down. Each agreed to pay half the lawyers' bills. Mälzel then invented something far more useful than the Panharmonicon — the **metronome**. Beethoven made a public announcement about how valuable the new device was and put metronome markings on his scores. This invention made Mälzel rich and he left Vienna for America.

Beat that! — An early metronome, which soon became an indispensable musical tool.

The Final Struggle

In 1814, encouraged by the success of his *Wellington's Victory* concert, Beethoven decided to look again at the manuscript of *Fidelio*. Working closely with theatre manager Georg Treitschke, who had a far better understanding than the composer of how to make things work well on stage, Beethoven cut, revised and re-wrote extensively — including yet another version of the opening overture. This time *Fidelio* was a great success and 20 performances were given, bringing Beethoven financial success.

The presence in Vienna of the leaders of Europe, gathered together to settle the affairs of the continent after the defeat of Napoleon, led Beethoven to give five major concerts. He used the resulting cash to buy shares in a bank. He was fortunate to be able to make some provision for his old age because public taste was turning away from his kind of music. Kinsky had already died, Lichnowsky died in 1814 and Lobkowitz in 1816. After the horrors of war, people seemed to want gay waltzes and the lively comic operas of the young Italian, Gioacchino Rossini, who was now the toast of Vienna. Beethoven was not interested in writing that kind of music and entered a long period of musical barrenness, plagued by family problems.

In November 1815, Carl Caspar Beethoven knew that he was dying.

Rossini (1792-1868) — he retired at 37 but lived to be 76, spending his great earnings on travel and entertaining.

He wanted to divide his property between his wife Johanna, and his brother Ludwig, and make them jointly responsible for bringing up his son, Karl. Ludwig protested that he did not "wish to be bound up with such a bad woman in a matter of such importance as the education of a child". The result was a family tug-of-war which was to last for the rest of Beethoven's life and bring great unhappiness to all concerned.

Beethoven genuinely wanted what was best for young Karl, but he had no experience of being a parent and by constantly changing his mind about what *was* best for him, prevented Karl from finding a steady way of life.

Karl was caught between a mother and an uncle who disliked and distrusted each other and argued constantly, each claiming to be acting in his best interests. In 1818, Johanna took Beethoven to court to get custody of her son and in 1819 she got it. A year later, Beethoven appealed to a higher court, and with the help of Archduke Rudolph, regained his nephew.

These years of anxiety took their toll on Beethoven's health. He was now drinking a whole bottle of wine with every meal. He did not become a drunkard like his father, but it was liver damage that would eventually kill him. Family and money worries also distracted him from composing. People began to say that he had simply lost his gift. But in fact he was slowly struggling with several massive works at once, including his *Missa Solemnis* (1818-1823) and Ninth Symphony (completed 1823). By now he at last understood how his own mind worked, musically speaking:

"I carry my thoughts about with me for a long time ... before I set them down ... my memory is so faithful to me that I am sure not to forget a theme which I have once conceived, even after years have passed. I make many changes, reject and re-attempt until I am satisfied. Then the working-out begins in my head ... It rises, grows upwards, and I hear and see the picture as a whole take shape and stand before me as though cast in a single piece, so that all that is left is the work of writing it down." Mozart's genius seemed effortless, as though he could conjure music out of the air. Beethoven's great works, by contrast, were produced by long, hard thought and effort, through which he considered and rejected every alternative way of expressing the effects he wanted to achieve. The result is a perfection which can be damaged by attempting to alter it, even slightly.

Battling for years with long, complex works meant that there was no regular income for Beethoven. He began to worry constantly about money, although he actually had quite enough of it if only he had been able to keep better track of it.

In 1819, Beethoven's old friend, Archduke Rudolph, was appointed Cardinal Archbishop of Olmütz in Moravia. A great ceremony was planned for 1820, when he would officially take up his appointment. Beethoven offered to write a special mass for the event, but, once he started, just could not seem to get it right. He finally finished it in 1823. Archduke Rudolph was not surprised by this and, when at last he heard the *Missa Solemnis*, he certainly wasn't disappointed.

The other great work of this period was Beethoven's Ninth Symphony, which represented the thoughts of over 30 years. Earlier, in 1793, Beethoven had told his friends that he would like to set the poet Schiller's *Ode to Joy* to music. The theme of the poem, the brotherhood of all men, seemed to Beethoven to express the best hopes of those revolutionary times. And, despite all the frustrations and disappointments that followed, the inspiration of the poem stayed with Beethoven throughout his life. He began working on the Ninth Symphony in 1812 and in 1818 suddenly thought of incorporating a choral movement, something no one had ever done before, using the *Ode to Joy* for its words.

The Ninth Symphony and the *Missa Solemnis* were performed for the first time at a concert in Vienna on 7 May, 1824. The audience responded enthusiastically but Beethoven, intent on watching the orchestra, was too deaf to notice and had to be turned round to face them before he could literally see the wild applause which he could no longer hear. It was to be his last public triumph and, sadly, the celebratory dinner afterwards was ruined when Beethoven accused one of the three organizers of the concert of cheating him over the takings. So all three walked out.

In 1822, Beethoven had patched up his 10 year quarrel with his brother Nikolaus Johann. In 1824, he reconciled himself to his sister-in-law Johanna as well, sending her money when she fell ill. But he still couldn't seem to improve his relationship with Karl. Karl, now 18 years old, was studying at the University of Vienna and also helping as his uncle's secretary, but Beethoven still treated him like a naughty boy, checking up on him all the time. Karl decided to join the army as the best way to get away from his uncle's constant interference. Beethoven wouldn't stand for the idea but did allow him to transfer to the Polytechnic Institute to study business. The army would almost certainly have sent Karl away somewhere, but Beethoven planned to set him up in a business after graduation so that he could keep him close by.

Beethoven was by now working on what were to be his last major compositions — a series of string quartets, commissioned by the Russian Prince Nikolas Galitzin in 1823. He was planning other works as well — oratorios like Handel's, a requiem mass, an overture in honour of Bach and a tenth symphony. But none of these ever got beyond the stage of being sketched out. The quartets, which are now regarded as being among Beethoven's greatest works, were a mystery to most people who heard them at the time. Prince Galitzin ran into money problems and never even paid for the compositions, but Beethoven remained unconcerned. He knew that he was now writing for posterity.

The composer's health continued to get worse, and early in 1826 he had to take to his bed for some

A calm portrait of the turbulent young Karl von Beethoven.

weeks. Karl's wild behaviour only made things worse. He neglected his studies, got drunk and ran up debts. Worse still, he kept lying to Beethoven and publicly referred to him as "the old fool". Then in July came terrible news — Karl had tried to shoot himself. Bleeding from a wound in the head, he had been carried to his mother's house to be nursed back to life. Beethoven was shattered by the near-tragedy and agreed at last to let Karl join the army.

In September 1826, nephew and uncle went off together for a restful spell at Nikolaus Johann's country estate at Gneizendorf. Beethoven carried on composing — and quarrelling, with Karl, and with Nikolaus Johann, and his wife. In December he insisted on returning to Vienna. The two day ride in an open carriage made him so ill he had to call for a doctor immediately on his return. He survived an attack of pneumonia but was then afflicted by liver failure. Karl dutifully looked after his uncle until he had to leave to join the army on 2 January.

Beethoven tried to work on his Tenth symphony and was greatly heartened by a surprise gift from London — a newly printed edition of Handel's complete works in 40 volumes. Beethoven declared "I can still learn from him", and wrote to his old friend Wegeler in Bonn "I hope still to bring some great works into the world". But his last battle was nearly over and on 23 March, 1827 he signed his will, leaving everything to Karl.

For the last three days of his life, Beethoven lay either unconscious or delirious. On the afternoon of 26 March a dreadful storm lashed the city. A tremendous clap of thunder roused the dying man to his senses. He opened his eyes and half rose from the pillows, eyes staring, fist clenched in a wordless gesture of defiance. Then he slumped back, dead.

On the afternoon of Beethoven's funeral, schools were closed and 10,000 people turned out to follow his coffin. Among them was the young composer, Franz Schubert, who was himself to die and be buried near to his **mentor** the following year. The funeral procession took an hour and a half to pass the few hundred yards from Beethoven's lodgings to the church. Famous singers carried the coffin. At the graveside an address was given, written by the poet Franz Grillparzer, in praise of the man mourned by an empire which honoured music above all the arts:

"he was an artist, and all that was his, was through his art alone ... He who comes after him will not continue him; he must begin anew ..."

But Beethoven had already written his own **epitaph** in one of his notebooks:

"What more can be given to man than fame and praise and immortality?"

The inscription on his headstone was even simpler. It read – "Beethoven". No-one would ever need to be told who he was.

Beethoven's headstone (above). **Note the bee, a symbol of industriousness. Capital tribute — Beethoven's funeral** (below).

Beethoven and Britain

As Beethoven lost his youthful admiration for revolutionary France he grew more and more fond of Britain. British music-lovers were among his warmest admirers, expressing their appreciation of his work most generously.

George Thomson of Edinburgh paid Beethoven over £500 for writing accompaniments for 150 traditional Scottish and Welsh songs. In 1818, the firm of Broadwood sent him one of their finest grand pianos, which he kept until his death. (It later belonged to the pianist Franz Liszt.) The Philharmonic Society offered the composer large fees to come to London and conduct a concert of his own works. He agreed but, nervous about the long journey, never actually kept his promise. He did, however, send them the score of his Ninth Symphony, inscribed "Written for the Philharmonic Society in London". As he lay dying, the Society sent him a gift of £100, a gesture from "the generous Englishmen", which touched him greatly.

Topping the Bill — Beethoven's great 8th Symphony, performed in London two years before his death.

UNDER THE IMMEDIATE PATRONAGE OF

His Majesty.

PHILHARMONIC SOCIETY.

THIRD CONCERT, MONDAY, MARCH 21, 1825.

ACT I.

Sinfonia Letter T. - - - - - - - *Haydn.*
Terzetto, "Tutte le mie speranze," Madame CARADORI, Miss GOODALL, and
  Mr. VAUGHAN (Davide Penitente) - - - - - *Mozart.*
Quartetto, two Violins, Viola, and Violoncello, Messrs. SPAGNOLETTI, OURY,
  MORALT, and LINDLEY - - - - - *Mozart.*
Song, Mr. VAUGHAN, "Why does the God of Israel sleep," (Samson) - *Handel.*
Quintetto, Flute, Oboë, Clarinet, Horn, and Bassoon, Messrs. NICHOLSON,
  VOGT, WILLMAN, PLATT, and MACKINTOSH - - - *Reicha.*
Recit. ed Aria, Madame CARADORI, "Per pietà," (Così fan tutte) - *Mozart.*
Overture, Les deux Journées - - - - - - *Cherubini.*

ACT II.

New Grand Characteristic Sinfonia, MS. with Vocal Finale, the principal
  parts of which to be sung by Madame CARADORI, Miss GOODALL,
  Mr. VAUGHAN, and Mr. PHILLIPS (composed expressly for this Society) - *Beethoven.*

Leader, Mr. F. CRAMER.—Conductor, Sir G. SMART.

Find out More

Important Books

The Beethoven Companion by Denis Arnold and Nigel Fortune (Faber, 1971)

Beethoven: Letters, Journals and Conversations by M. Hamburger (Thames & Hudson, 1984)

The New Grove Beethoven by Joseph L. Kerman and Alan Tyson (1983)

Beethoven by Denis Matthews (Dent, 1985)

Beethoven by Ates Orga (Omnibus Press, 1983)

Play Beethoven by Alison Sage (Octopus Books, 1988)

Beethoven & His Nephew by R. Sterba and E. Sterba (Dobson Books, 1981)

Beethoven and England by Pamela J. Willetts (British Library, 1970)

Important Dates

1770 Born in Bonn
1775 Begins to study music
1781 Ends formal schooling
1784 Appointed second organist at Bonn court
1787 Meets Mozart in Vienna
1789 Named as head of the family
1790 Meets Joseph Haydn
1792 Moves to Vienna; death of his father
1795 Makes concert debut
1800 Completes First symphony; first public concert
1801 Onset of deafness; completes *Moonlight Sonata*
1802 Writes Heiligenstadt Testament; completes Second symphony
1803 House composer at Theater-an-der-Wien
1804 Finishes third symphony, *Eroica*
1805 First performance of *Fidelio* (1st version)

1808 Completes sixth symphony, *Pastoral*; gives last solo public performance
1809 Granted an annuity by aristocratic patrons; French occupy Vienna
1813 Writes *Wellington's Victory*
1814 Plays piano for the last time in public
1816 Takes over guardianship of his nephew, Karl
1819 Becomes totally deaf
1820 Wins final guardianship of Karl
1822 Abandons last attempt at conducting
1824 Triumphant performance of *Missa Solemnis* and Ninth Symphony
1826 Karl attempts suicide
1827 Beethoven dies

Glossary

Armistice   An agreement signed between countries at war in order to stop the fighting.

Cantata   A musical composition originally with one spoken voice and a solo instrument. Today it can also mean a choral work for concert performances.

Counterpoint   The art of combining different melodies.

Epitaph   A short composition written to honour the memory of someone who has died.

Florin   An old silver coin.

Mentor   A tutor or trainer.

Metronome   An instrument which can be set to beat so many times a minute giving the right speed for a piece of music.

Misanthropic   A hating or distrusting of mankind.

Patron   Somebody who supports another person either through money or influence.

Pockmark   The mark or scar made by spots caused by diseases such as smallpox.

Sonata   A musical composition of three or four movements, written for piano or for a solo instrument with piano accompaniment.

Snuff   A powdered mixture of tobacco which used to be placed on the back of the hand and inhaled.

Symphony   The name given to an elaborate and serious composition written for a full orchestra.

Virtuoso   A musician who is very technically skilled in the art.

Index

Albrechtsberger, Johann Georg 9

Beethoven, Carl Caspar 8,10,20,21,24
Beethoven, Johann van 5,6,8,9,10
Beethoven, Karl 21, 24, 26,27
Beethoven, Ludwig van
    birth 5
    finishes school 7
    becomes second organist 7
    plays for Mozart 7
    first visit to Vienna 7
    takes control of family 8
    returns to Vienna 10
    goes on tour 11
    first work published 12
    first symphony published 12
    first public concert 13
    hearing difficulties begin 13
    writes "Heiligenstadt Testament" 14
    completes second symphony 15
    completes *Eroica* 16
    writes only opera 17
    birth of nephew 21
    proposes marriage 21
    regains custody of nephew 25
    finishes *Missa Solemnis* 25
    last public performance 26
    dies 27
Beethoven, Ludwig van (grandfather) 4,5,6
Beethoven, Maria Josepha 5
Beethoven, Nikolaus Johann 8,10,21,26
Bonaparte, Jerome 19,20
Bonaparte, Napoleon 16,22,24,27
Bonn 4,8
Britain 29

Cantata 8,31
Christ on the Mount of Olives 17
Counterpoint 9,31
Czerny, Carl 13,14

Emperor Joseph II 8
Eroica 16
Esterhazy, Prince Nikolaus 19

Family von Breuning 7,8
Fidelio 17,18,24
First symphony 12
Förster, Emanuel Aloys 9
France 10,11,16,20,29

Galitzin, Prince Nikolaus 26
Grillparzer, Franz 28

Haydn, Joseph 8,9,10,16,19
Heiligenstadt 14

Kinsky, Prince 20,24

Leonore 17,18
Lichnowsky, Prince Carl 11,15,17,18,24
Liszt, Franz 13,29
Lobkowitz, Prince 16,20,24

Malfatti, Therese 21
Malzel, Johann 22,23
"Mechanical Panharmonican" 22
Metronome 23
Missa Solemnis 25
Mozart, Wolfgang Amadeus 7,10,11,12,16

Neefe, Christian Gottlob 7,9
Ninth Symphony 25

Patron 4,10,16
Philharmonic Society, The 29

Reiss, Johanna 21,24,26
Ries, Ferdinand 14
Rossini, Gioacchino 24
Rudolph, Archduke 19,20,25

Salieri, Antonio 9
Schenk, Johann 9
Schiller 26
Schubert, Franz 27
Second Symphony 15

Theater-an-der-Wien 17
Third Symphony 16
Treitschke, Georg 24

Ulm, battle of 18

Vienna 7,8,9,10
Virtuoso 7,31
Vittoria, battle of 22

Waldstein, Count Ferdinand 8,10
Wegeler, Franz 14
Wellington, Duke of 22

Picture Acknowledgements

The publishers would like to thank the following for their kind permission to reproduce their photographs in this book: Austrian National Library, Vienna 27; Beethoven House Archives, Bonn frontispiece, 4, 5 (top left), 6,7,11,12,15,17,20, 21, 28; Mary Evans Picture Library cover, 5 (top right), 8,9,10,16,18,19,22,23,24; Royal College of Music 13,29,31.